Dear Reader,

So, what *is* "real beauty"? Real beauty is celebrating the girl *you* are. It's the knowledge that you like yourself and that you're true to your own heart. It's having eyes that sparkle with compassion and see the best in people. It's having lips that speak strongly when you're pushed around and gently when someone else has been. It's taking good care of yourself inside and out.

The most beautiful trait you can have is confidence! Figure out what you like best about yourself and let it shine. *That's* what real beauty is all about.

Your friends at American Girl

Louisburg Library
Bringing People and Information Together

contents

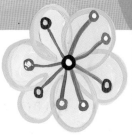

real
beauty

No one's smile shines exactly like yours.

1 List **five words to describe yourself.**

The trick—do not describe any physical features and use words other than "nice"! Some creative words to choose from could be:

strong

bright

loving

fast

smart

scientific

artistic

assertive

rare

playful

studious

warm

dramatic

goofy

kind

sensitive

silly

hardworking

funny

curious

helpful

adventurous

thoughtful

musical

generous

joyful

unique

easygoing

I am . . .

1. _____

2. _____

3. _____

4. _____

5. _____

daring

quick

friendly

brave

patient

2

Praise people for what they can do, not just for how they look. Compliment a friend today on something other than her appearance.

3

This week, ask your mom or grandmother how she felt about her appearance when she was your age. What does she know now that she wishes she'd known then?

When you accomplish something you're really proud of—whether it's passing a tough test or finishing a winning soccer season—*that's* when you're at your most beautiful. Give yourself a pat on the back! Call a grandparent or e-mail a favorite aunt to share the news. Celebrate with family or friends.

5

Limit your face time. It's O.K. to give yourself a once-over in the mirror before you head out in the morning.

☑ Face washed?

☑ Fly zipped?

☑ Hair not standing straight up (unless you like it that way)?

It's fine to want to see what's changing and to daydream about who you're becoming. But spending too much time in front of the mirror—or peeking at your reflection in every window you pass—is not worth it. You've got better things to do!

6 **Really** accept a compliment. When a friend says, "You look great," don't brush her off with "I think these pants make me look goofy." Just say, **"Thanks,"** and let the words sink in.

7 It's natural to wonder how other people see you, but remember, **you're** the final judge of how you look. Don't fish for compliments. When you ask, "Do I look O.K.?" you're putting your appearance out for judgment.

Some girls say they think they're not pretty because they want people to insist they are. The best way to feel pretty is to be confident!
Maddy, age 11, Oklahoma

body basics

**Your body is a gift of great value.
Treat it as though it's the
most valuable thing you have—
it is!**

Everyone's body is changing—take interest in what's happening to yours. Read books. Ask teachers. Talk to Mom.

Knowledge is power.

Celebrate taking care of yourself.

Take time today to pamper your skin with a great-smelling soap or lotion. Clean and cut your fingernails.

Have a dancer's poise. Imagine there's a thread attached to the center of the top of your head. Now imagine someone is pulling gently on that thread to make you stand up tall and straight. Try to keep your poise all day long!

10

11

Even if you wake up feeling lousy—or just lazy—wash your face, comb your hair, brush your teeth, and get dressed. **Give your body respect,** and you'll get respect from the rest of the world, too.

12

Be prepared! Keep an emergency kit tucked away in your backpack. It can hold antiperspirant, pimple cream, a sanitary napkin or tampon, a couple of Band-Aids, and emergency phone numbers. You'll feel better knowing that you're prepared if your face flares up or your period starts.

13

Try a sports bra. When you put one on, you can't help it—you feel like a member of the U.S. Women's Soccer Team! Take time to try on different styles, and see which one feels like the best fit for your body.

P.S. If you're big chested, look for a version with a racer back and underwire shaping. It will offer more support and won't squeeze as tightly as a stretchy compression-style bra.

14

Smart girls know that even features that bug them have bright sides.

I don't like being short, but my other short friends and I call each other "fun size"—like the little candy bars!
Cary, age 11, New York

I have to get braces—again!—really soon because I'm missing some of my adult teeth. I don't like my teeth, but I know they'll look good when all the orthodontics stuff is done.
Ashley, age 11, South Carolina

I have freckles and sometimes I don't like them because it looks like there are spots on my face. But other times I think they make me look cute.
Beatrice, age 9, New York

My hair is unruly and curly! It gets kind of annoying sometimes, because it looks the same every day. When I have time to fix it, it looks pretty. I like that it's different from everybody else's hair.

Kristin, age 13, Kentucky

I don't like having to wear glasses, but a lot of celebrities who don't need them wear them because they think they're stylish.

Olga, age 13, Massachusetts

Write something good about a feature you sometimes don't like.

_____

_____

_____

_____

_____

_____

15

List three things you like about your looks.
When you're having a bad day, focus on what you like about yourself.

1. _____

2. _____

3. _____

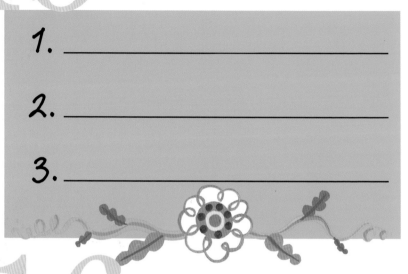

16

Tired of having tinsel teeth? Look around at all your friends who have braces, too. Visualize how great all your smiles will be when your braces come off!

17

Feeling uncoordinated? Remember that your body is growing and changing, so **it's normal to be klutzy at times.** Slow down a little. Don't call yourself names. And if you trip or mess up in gym class, laugh at yourself and try again.

big
TRUTH

18

On some days your clothes will fit tighter than on others. It's normal for your body to change. You gain a little; you lose a little. That's the way bodies work.

Don't waste time comparing yourself to others. There's no one out there just like you, who has grown up with your experiences and has your talents.

Listen to your body when you play sports. Don't push yourself past your body's limits, even if you're told to toughen up. Your instincts will tell you when to stop.

Buy whatever size of clothing fits you most comfortably. Don't get hung up on the number on the label. Label sizes are not consistent. A size 9 from one brand might fit like a 7 from another, so don't be surprised if you fit into a wide range of sizes.

healthy
eating

Get a good food attitude.
Notice which meals make you feel
healthy, strong, and satisfied. Did you
know that your body usually feels best
when you eat a meal that includes foods
of different colors, tastes, textures,
and temperatures? Remember that
food is fuel—it keeps your body moving.

22 quiz:

Are You a Healthy Eater?

To keep your body revved up, eat a healthy diet that provides the sources of energy, vitamins, and minerals your body needs—especially as you grow and change. Are you a healthy eater? Find out by taking this quiz. Put a ✓ next to each item you can answer positively:

At each meal, I make sure to eat some source of:

☐ **protein** for my muscles.

Protein is found in beef, milk, tofu, beans, peanut butter, fish, chicken, pork, eggs, and cheese.

☐ **vitamins** so my body can grow, heal, and make energy.

You get vitamins from fruits, vegetables, meat, whole grains, and dairy products.

☐ **calcium** so my bones grow and stay strong.

Milk, cottage cheese, yogurt, cheese, salmon, and dark green veggies are good sources of calcium.

☐ **carbohydrates** to provide my body with the energy it needs to be active.

Potatoes, peas, corn, beans, whole grains, tortillas, pasta, and bread are all high-carb foods.

☐ **fat** so my body has healthy cell walls and membranes.

Fat can be found in olives, avocado, nuts, salad dressing, oils, and butter.

How did you do? To be a healthy eater, aim for a check mark next to every item above.

23

Watch your serving sizes the next time you eat out. "Super sizes" are often three times more food than you need to be healthy. When you get home, eat a piece of fruit and a veggie to supply your body with the nutrients missing from most fast-food meals.

24

Skip soda pop and juice—drink water! Carry a water bottle and try to drink at least 32 ounces each day.

25 Take your time when you eat.

It takes a while for your brain to get the message from your stomach that you're full. Plus, the more slowly you chew and the more you focus on each bite, the more flavorful your food tastes.

26 Make a meal something special.

Even if you're only having cereal for breakfast with your little brother, create traditions to make the moment memorable. Set the table. Take turns sharing funny dreams from the night before. At dinner, have a parent light a candle for the table. Enjoy giving yourself the fuel you need and sharing your ideas and feelings with the people eating with you.

27

Learn what hunger feels like. Your body sends out a unique combination of sensations when you're hungry and need food for fuel. Your stomach might churn or gurgle. Your mouth might water. You might feel tired or get a headache. Try to remember a time when you were really hungry—maybe you got so busy that you had to eat lunch a few hours later than usual. How did it feel to be **physically** hungry?

28 It's easy to get feelings of physical hunger mixed up with feelings of boredom, anxiety, loneliness, or excitement. When you think you're hungry, ask yourself, "What am I *really* hungry for?" Food satisfies only physical hunger. If you're actually craving a big hug or a break from studying, that's *heart hunger.*  Instead of eating, go snuggle with your dog or set aside your homework for ten minutes to play a quick game of cards with Mom.

Go on a **food safari!** Eating new kinds of food is fun—and good for you. The greater the variety of foods you eat, the greater the variety of nutrients you give your body. The next time someone in your family goes grocery shopping, go along and explore each aisle. What do you see that you've never tasted before? What new food

might you like to try? Ask your parents if you can buy one item you've never tried before—like a star fruit or mango— and give it a taste test at home.

30

If your friends start talking about their weight or diet, change the subject.

Show them there are more interesting things to talk about!

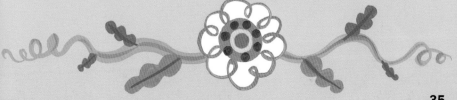

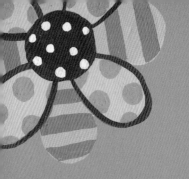

31
quiz:

Aim to be **healthy,** not skinny. Use this checklist
to notice how you treat your body. Put a  ✓ next to
each item with which you can agree.

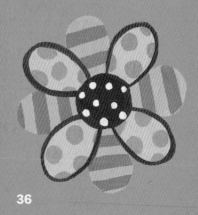

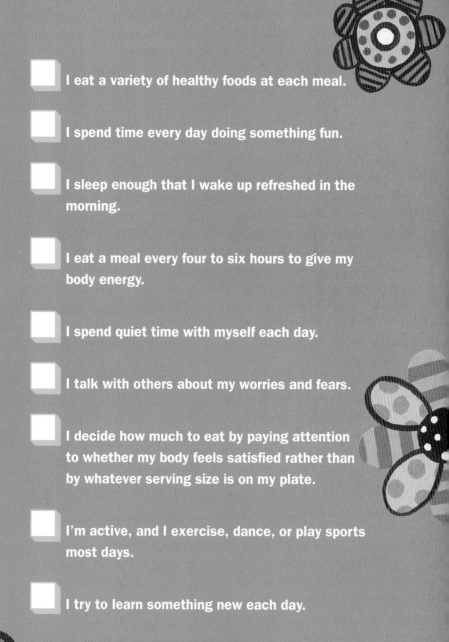

☐ I eat a variety of healthy foods at each meal.

☐ I spend time every day doing something fun.

☐ I sleep enough that I wake up refreshed in the morning.

☐ I eat a meal every four to six hours to give my body energy.

☐ I spend quiet time with myself each day.

☐ I talk with others about my worries and fears.

☐ I decide how much to eat by paying attention to whether my body feels satisfied rather than by whatever serving size is on my plate.

☐ I'm active, and I exercise, dance, or play sports most days.

☐ I try to learn something new each day.

mood makeovers

Feelings come and go,
like the tide in the ocean.
The best way to change your mood
is to send positive attention
to your body.

big
TRUTH

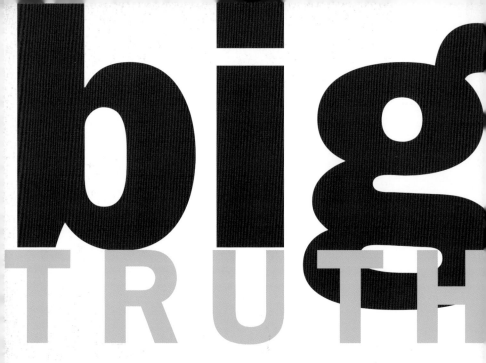

It's **O.K.** to not feel perky or peppy all the time. Sometimes you have to live with the bad feelings and just know that they'll pass. If you feel seriously sad, though, be sure to talk to an adult who cares about you.

33

When you're in a bad mood, your body knows it. Think about which part of your body gets out of whack when you're crabby or upset. Do you get a stomachache when you're nervous about a test? Do you get a headache when you feel anxious? If you recognize your body's signals, you may be able to figure out what's bothering you and make yourself feel better.

34

Life seems much harder when you're short on sleep! The average 10- to 12-year-old needs 9 ¾ to 10 hours of sleep a night. Take a nap—even a short one can leave you feeling refreshed.

35

Need to **brighten your mood?** If it's daytime, open the window and let in some fresh air and sunlight. If it's nighttime, put on clean pj's and curl up with a favorite book, movie, or CD.

36

Play, cuddle, or walk with your pet. If you don't have a pet of your own, borrow one from a neighbor or friend and enjoy some playtime together.

37

Feeling stressed? Take a warm bath or shower. Imagine the water washing away your worries.

38

Learn deep breathing.
Your breath connects all parts
of you—your body, mind, and
spirit. Breathing from your
belly instead of your chest
can be very relaxing.

Try this deep-breathing exercise: Lie on your back and place a paperback book (like this one!) just below your navel. When you inhale, think of the breath traveling through your chest and deep into your belly.

As you inhale, say to yourself "in" and notice that the book rises slightly. As you exhale, softly say to yourself "out" and notice as the book lowers. Try not to force the book up and down.

Enjoy the relaxation between breaths, and if your mind wanders, bring it back to focus on the rhythm of your words and your breathing.

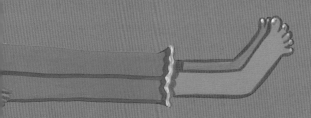

39

Create your own peace rituals. When you're angry or stressed out, take three long, slow, deep breaths. Write in your journal. Turn on your favorite music. Find ways to calm your spirit, and return to those practices whenever you feel anxious.

When you're having a bad day, **ask for help.** Tell a close friend if you're feeling sad. Let Mom know if you're worried about your English paper. Ask Dad for a hug. The support of a friend or family member can feel like a blanket of strength wrapped around your shoulders.

41

Try yoga. The stretching and meditation involved in yoga can help you feel peaceful and powerful. Here's a great pose to do when your legs are tired from playing soccer or standing all day long. Start with your shoes off!

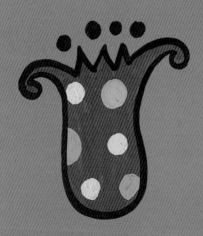

1. Fold a blanket into a rectangle about two feet wide and several inches thick. Place the blanket about six inches away from a wall, with the short end facing the wall.

2. Sit with the right side of your body against the wall. Exhale and, with a smooth movement, swing your legs up, swivel your rear end toward the wall and your back toward the blanket, and gently lower your head and shoulders down. Your heels should be resting on the wall and your knees slightly bent. Your feet and legs should be relaxed.

3. Lie there for one to five minutes and relax. Feel the sensation of the blood flowing toward your heart.

4. To come out of the pose, bend your knees and slowly push back off the blanket. Then roll onto your right side and rest for about 30 seconds. Notice how alive your legs feel!

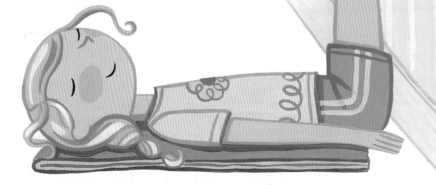

42

It's normal to feel mad sometimes, but it's important to handle your anger in a healthy way. When you're home stewing about a fight with a friend, take a minute and picture yourself talking calmly with her. Practice saying "I feel mad when you _____" and fill in the reason. When you've settled down, talk to your friend for real. Remember, stay calm and focus on the issue. It's not fair to bring up problems from yesterday, last week, or last year.

43

Ask a friend you trust to be your **Pep-Talk Partner (PTP).** A PTP is someone you can call when you're down or when your spirit needs a boost. As a partner, of course, you'll do the same for your friend when she needs help.

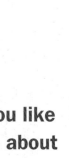

44

Try this with your PTP: Write down **three things you like** about **yourself** and **three things you like about** your **friend.** Have her do the same thing, then trade papers and compare. Did she like the same things about you that you did? What did you learn about yourself and each other?

45

Make your space beautiful.

Clean your room. Organize. It's hard to be peaceful when you're surrounded by chaos. A calm, orderly room can make you feel better about yourself. Plus you'll be able to find the clothes you want, and they won't be rolled up in a wad under your bed!

Hang artwork you've made yourself on the closet door or a bulletin board. Frame your favorite piece and show it off in a sunny spot.

47 Make a happy corner—a place to display birthday cards, notes from Grandma, valentines from friends, or anything else that reminds you how many people care about you.

48 Make sure that the photo collection in your room includes a picture of yourself that you really like.

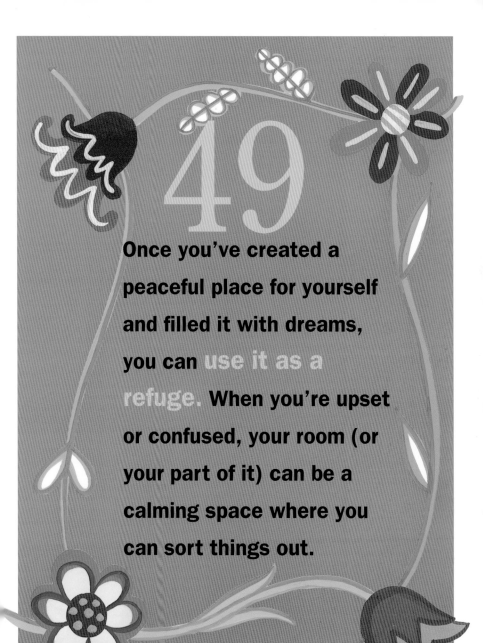

49

Once you've created a peaceful place for yourself and filled it with dreams, you can use it as a refuge. When you're upset or confused, your room (or your part of it) can be a calming space where you can sort things out.

life skills

Dream big. Set goals. Be good at something—then get better at it! Be proud of yourself. Teach others, and never, ever stop learning.

50

Start a dream list. Find a pretty notebook and write down places you'd like to visit, experiences you'd like to have, people you'd like to meet, and skills you'd like to learn. A dream list is a great start to creating a life filled with fun, adventure, and interesting experiences. Put a box next to each item on your list so you can check it off when it happens.

51

Be proud when you're good at something.

If you do a great back walkover, more power to you! What's the difference between being proud and bragging? It's all about timing.

If you want to show your friends your skill, pick an appropriate moment to do so—not during class or when people are focused on something else. When you're hanging out sometime, first ask your friends if they want to see what you've mastered. Then give it all you've got. Make sure you compliment other people on what they do well, too.

52

Can you juggle, shuffle cards, or swing a baseball bat like nobody's business? **Teach** your mother, your little brother, or a friend one of your special skills. It feels good to be an expert! Be patient and give your pupil lots of encouragement. Remember what it was like when you were first learning?

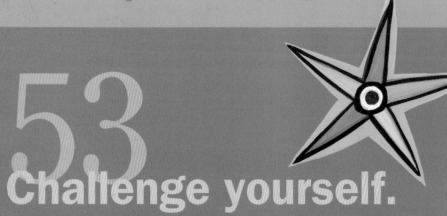

53 Challenge yourself.

Do you play an instrument? Play a song that's more difficult than usual or learn a tune by ear—no sheet music allowed. Do you like to run? Run a little farther than you usually go. Raise the bar for yourself—then leap it!

Identify your "cheer squad."

Your personal cheer squad is made up of people who support, encourage, and want what's best for you. Write down the names of three of your "cheerleaders," and describe how each has helped you. Then write each one a note, send her an e-mail, or give her a call to thank her for her encouragement. Go, team!

1._____

2._____

3._____

55 Laugh

till your
stomach hurts

(even if it makes you snort!).

List five things you're good at, whether it's math or making up jokes. If you feel down about yourself, check out this list, and remember—you rock!

1. _____

2. _____

3. _____

4. _____

5. _____

Instead of trying to change your looks, figure out the inner qualities and talents that make you special. You'll feel good inside and out.

Kara, age 12, Oregon

57

If standing up for yourself is hard to do, ask your mom to look into a **self-defense course** that's appropriate for girls your age. You'll be amazed at how learning to defend yourself against someone twice your size will make your confidence soar.

move it and groove it

Get out of breath. Chase the dog.
Shoot hoops. Throw a Frisbee.
Roll down a hill. Do a cartwheel.
Isn't it amazing how many things
your body can do?

58 Turn off the TV and **go play.** Exercise doesn't have to be hard work—it can be a social time for you and your friends. Grab your best bud and go in-line skating. Walk to the park to swing. Play a CD and dance. You'll definitely feel better than if you'd stayed stuck to the sofa.

59

List at least five physical things your body does well, such as:

water-ski

skip

kick a
soccer ball

twirl a
hula hoop

read a street sign
a block away
without glasses

Write them all down!

1. _____

2. _____

3. _____

4. _____

5. _____

What you can **do** is more important than what size you wear.

60

Try something new! Don't avoid trying a new activity just because you're not good at it! How do you think you *get* good? By doing it over and over and over again.

In fact, if you want to do anything well, you have to be willing to do it poorly at the beginning. This week, try one thing you've been afraid to do because you might flop. You don't have to be a superstar. It's O.K. to just be O.K.

Find a role model **for your favorite physical activity, whether it's tennis, running, or stilt-walking. Look for someone—a relative, friend, or neighbor—who shares your interest. Ask for advice. Learn, then try it out.**

Feeling mad? Sweat it out. **Exercise is a great way to get rid of pent-up anger. Swim. Skate. Throw a softball with a friend (no, not AT a friend—WITH a friend).**

63

Make a **Move-It-Groove-It CD.** Burn a CD or make a tape filled only with songs that lift your spirits or get you moving. When you hit "play," open the windows and sing along—loud!

64

Dance. If your brother laughs at you, keep dancing—and sing while you're at it.

Fact or Fiction?

A quiz from girlpower.gov*

1. Girls who play sports do better in school.

Fact   Fiction

2. Physical activity improves your mood.

Fact   Fiction

3. A diet low in fat and high in vitamins and minerals, combined with regular physical activity, can keep you healthier.

Fact   Fiction

4. Girls involved in athletics are less likely to use drugs.

Fact   Fiction

5. Exercising when you're young may decrease your risk of getting breast cancer as an adult.

   Fact   Fiction

6. A girl who plays sports is less likely to put up with an abusive relationship.

   Fact   Fiction

7. Physical activity doesn't have to be strenuous to be effective.

   Fact   Fiction

8. Eating right and exercising now (and for the rest of your life) may mean a brighter future for you.

   Fact   Fiction

*Girl Power and girlpower.gov is a national campaign sponsored by the U.S. Department of Health and Human Services to help encourage and motivate 9- to 13-year-old girls.

answers

1. **Fact.** Female athletes tend to do better academically, receive higher grades, and score higher on standardized tests.

The President's Council on Physical Fitness and Sports

Girls who play sports have a lower drop-out rate and are three times more likely to graduate from college.

The Women's Sports Foundation

2. **Fact.** Exercising three times a week or more can make you healthier, not only physically but mentally, too. That's because physical activity can boost your self-esteem, increase your self-confidence, and generally make you feel more positive about your body. Exercise may also help relieve the painful feelings that come with depression and anxiety.

The President's Council on Physical Fitness and Sports

3. **Fact.** Many health organizations have found that eating right and exercising can reduce your risk of heart disease, obesity, high blood pressure, some forms of cancer, and other health problems.

4. **Fact.** Girls who play sports are 92 percent less likely to use drugs than girls who aren't active during their teens.

The Women's Sports Foundation

5. **Fact.** Girls who exercise just two hours a week may reduce the risk of later getting breast cancer by 60 percent. Many medical experts agree that a diet that's high in fiber and vitamins and low in saturated fat may also help reduce your risk of breast cancer.

Nike's PLAY Foundation

6. **Fact.** Girls who play sports may be less likely to stand for abusive relationships, possibly because of the inner strength and self-respect they develop playing sports.

Nike's PLAY Foundation

7. **Fact.** If you can't do long, intense workouts, you can still get the benefits of exercise. Moderate physical activity each day—taking a brisk walk for half an hour or dancing like crazy around your bedroom for 15 minutes—can help build strong bones, muscles, and joints. It can also reduce body fat and increase lean muscle mass.

U.S. Surgeon General

8. **Fact.** Eating right and exercising give you:
- a better chance of staying healthy all your life.
- a more positive attitude about yourself.
- a stronger body and sharper mind.

style sense

Fashion can be fun if you
don't worry about what people think.
Choose clothes that express
who you are and what you like.

Wear clothes that make you feel good.

You know which shirt makes you feel self-conscious and which pants make you squirm. Talk to your mom about why you don't feel comfy in those clothes, and ask if you can give them to charity.

Wear your favorite color.
If you feel great in it, your confidence will show!

Don't try to be so-called "cool" or "normal"—
be yourself. My dad always says,
**"Normal is just a setting
on the dryer."**
Allison, age 12, Texas

68

If someone teases you about the clothes you wear, shrug it off and say, "Oh, well. What matters is that *I* like 'em!"

69

Wearing tiny T-shirts and itty-bitty shorts may get you attention—but people might not see the real you. Choose clothes that help you present the inner girl you want the world to see.

Do you need eyeglasses? When you
pick out frames with your parents, take
along a friend whose opinion you trust.
Second opinions help!
(It's hard to see yourself in the mirror.
You need glasses, remember?)

71 Try a new 'do. Brush your hair, braid it, twist it, and tie it. **Experiment!** You can express yourself through your appearance, and no one way is right. They're all you.

72 Getting your hair cut at a salon? If you don't know what kind of cut you want, **schedule extra time to talk with the stylist.** If the stylist has time to listen, understand, and help you find ideas, chances are better that you'll like what you get. P.S. Even if you end up not liking your hairstyle, remember: hair grows.

73 When you get your hair cut, tell the stylist **how much time you can spend on your hair** every day. Don't get a style that requires more time to do than you have to give!

One time I went to school with braids in my hair. Everyone in school was saying that my hair looked nice. Later, one of my friends came up and said I looked weird. I was about to take my braids out when my best friend said, "If you like your braids, you should keep them. Don't listen to other people. It's what you think that counts." I felt much better afterward.

Ashley, age 11, California

74

Develop your own style. Experiment with clothing to see what makes you feel best. Some days you may feel sparkly and fancy—other days you won't! That's O.K.

75

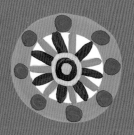

This week, visit a clothing store with a friend and pick out five outfits in colors and styles that you'd never consider wearing. Then **have fun** trying them on!

Don't be surprised if something you thought would look awful actually looks pretty good. Have a laugh at the outfits you don't like.

very! big
TRUTH

76

People aren't looking at you or talking about you nearly as much as you think they are.

clear thinking

Make up your own mind. There may be lots of people who want to help you make decisions. Listen to their advice (some of it might be good!) but make your own choices. Even if you make mistakes along the way, you'll know that the path you're taking is the right one for you.

77

Think of a person you admire. When you have a difficult decision to make and aren't sure which choice is right, ask yourself what your role model would do.

78

Are you an **independent thinker—or swayed by the crowd?** Circle the answer that best represents when you'd change something about your appearance:

a. If my best friend said I'd look better that way

b. If I thought it would make me more popular

c. If I wanted to experiment or try something new

d. If I thought my crush would like it

e. If the style was all the rage in magazines

Answer: If you circled any answer other than c, think twice about what—or who—is pushing you to change. The only good reason for changing something about your appearance is if it is healthier for you, or if you feel like experimenting with a new style. You can listen to other people's opinions, but don't let them sway your own.

79

If you feel like complaining about a situation, first think, *Is there anything I can do to make things better?* For example, if tempers flare one morning when everyone's rushing off to school and work, get yourself ready and then quietly see if you can help your little sister. **Help solve the problem** instead of contributing to the chaos.

big
TRUTH

80

Have you been hurt by words? Remember this: **People who insult others usually do it to make themselves feel powerful.** Know what that means? They're probably insecure. *They* are the ones who lack confidence, so try not to bend to the pressure to return their jabs with an insult.

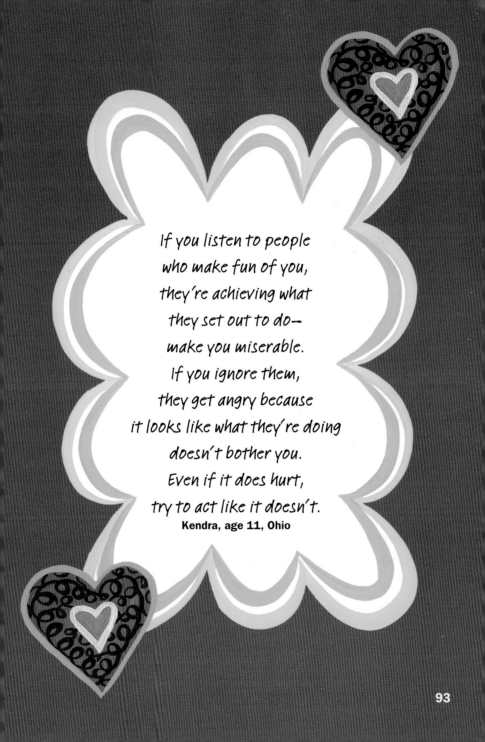

If you listen to people
who make fun of you,
they're achieving what
they set out to do—
make you miserable.
If you ignore them,
they get angry because
it looks like what they're doing
doesn't bother you.
Even if it does hurt,
try to act like it doesn't.

Kendra, age 11, Ohio

Break up a big goal into small steps. Baby steps + practicepracticepractice = accomplishment. Ta-da!

82

You can make a difference in the world. If you think you're too small to matter, think about what it feels like to have a pebble in your shoe. The pebble may be tiny, but it sure can get your attention!

reality check

Every day TV, movies, and magazines bombard you with their ideas of what a beautiful girl is supposed to look like. It's a runaway train of unrealistic images! Put on the brakes and jump off NOW. Beauty comes in all shapes and sizes.

83

The next time you're at the mall or in a crowded airport, take a look at all the **different kinds of bodies** out there. Then notice how few people are built like willowy, rail-thin models.

big
TRUTH

It's a celebrity's JOB to look a certain way. Did you know that singers, actresses, and models devote a good portion of their lives to their appearance? Most stars don't wake up looking like they stepped out of *Teen People*. They hire hairstylists and makeup artists to fuss with their faces. They pay trainers to help them exercise for hours a day. They hire wardrobe stylists to choose and fit their clothes. Photographers and cameramen may work all day to get that one photo where every hair is just the way they want it. That's the "casual" image you see in print or on-screen.

So when you see a star and think, "I wish I looked like her," remember this: Most of the day, *she* may not even look like her!

Don't believe everything you see.

Even after a celebrity's photo is taken, the work isn't done. High-tech experts use computers to touch up your favorite stars' images. They can change the shape of someone's body, get rid of a pimple, make teeth look whiter, and work all kinds of make-believe magic.

Challenge what you see.

If you don't like how girls are portrayed in a TV show, movie, or magazine, let the people in charge know! On the Internet, you can find addresses for every television network, movie studio, and magazine around. Write and tell the people in charge how you feel. Talk back!

87

Recognize stereotypes for what they are— uninformed judgments. Not all people with glasses are brainiacs. Not all redheads have fiery tempers. What other stereotypes do you see out there?

word power

Words are mighty, mighty things. The words you say to others—and to yourself—have incredible power. Choose them wisely.

Notice how many times a day you
say something that helps or encourages someone,
including yourself. That means saying things like:

Pay attention today. How many times did you encourage someone? Try to increase that number tomorrow.

Some mornings I really feel that I don't look my best, and when I feel that way I always have a bad day. So I started looking in the mirror and telling myself one thing that was good about me, other than looks. It's a great pick-me-up.

Brittany, age 14, New York

Speak up. If a family member makes you feel bad about how you look, let that person know. Does your mom call you a nickname, like Short Stuff or Chubby Cheeks, that makes you feel self-conscious? Sit down with her, calmly explain why you don't like the nickname, and ask her to stop using it.

big

TRUTH

90

Cruelty is always wrong. If someone—
a bully, a friend, or your big sister—insults you, and
you're tempted to come back with mean words of
your own, remember that being intentionally cruel
is always bad news.

But that's not saying you should take abuse. If someone is mean or tries to hurt you, speak up for yourself.
Say "Stop it!" Don't keep it a secret, either. Talk to a
teacher or a parent and let one of them help you come
up with ways to handle the problem.

91 If you're envious of a friend, don't let your feelings fester. Try acknowledging them in a compliment. When you express admiration, your envy usually fades away.

> Wow, you are so good at shooting free throws!

92 When a friend is better than you are at something, ask yourself what she's been willing to do that you have not. She may be a natural—but most likely she's a great free-throw shooter because she practices every day, even when it's not basketball season. You may choose to do other things with your time.

> If I want to be that good at shooting free throws, I need to work and spend time on it.

93

Say good-bye to extremes

such as "I never . . ." or "I always . . .". When you make a mistake, steer clear of saying "I never do that right" or "I always mess up." Chances are your goof was a one-time mistake. Tell yourself that *next* time, you'll know what to do.

94

Learn to speak your mind, even if you disagree with other people. Agreeing just to please someone means you're not being true to yourself. Don't worry that you're being impolite—you can disagree without being rude. Try words such as "I see your point, but I think . . .".

Your ideas matter.

be beauty-full

Beauty is as beauty DOES. Your actions and words, not your lip gloss, show the world who you really are.

95

You know the Golden Rule:

Treat people the way you want to be treated.

Follow it!

96

Follow the reverse Golden Rule, too:

Be as kind to yourself as you are to others.

If you're tempted to rip on your reflection in the mirror, ask yourself, *Would I say that to my best friend?*

97

Get cozy with your journal and write about these topics:

- three good things that happened to me today
- the nicest thing anyone ever said to me
- five things I'm grateful for
- a time I faced a tough situation and succeeded

98

Did you ever notice that when you criticize others, you end up feeling bad about yourself?

Insulting others insults your own spirit.

Don't go there!

Be creative!

Do a drawing for the street fair, learn to play an instrument, or make jewelry. Creativity makes your spirit soar.

100

Part One: Imagine that a friend or a younger cousin came to you and said, "I hate the way I look!" What advice would you give her?

Part Two: <u>Remember</u> that advice when you're feeling down about yourself.

I'm pretty happy the way I am. I don't really care about my appearance as long as I don't look like I have been through a natural disaster! It's what's on the inside that counts, not the outside.

Lindsey, age 11, North Carolina

big
TRUTH
101

Finding beauty in those around you gives YOU a more beautiful spirit.

What I believe:

☐ I feel good about myself.

☐ I am strong.

☐ I take care of my body.

☐ I try new things.

☐ I express my feelings.

☐ I am silly sometimes.

☐ I make mistakes, and that's O.K.

☐ I can change.

☐ I like being 100 percent ME.

Signed_____

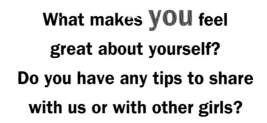

What makes **you** feel
great about yourself?
Do you have any tips to share
with us or with other girls?

Send your ideas to:
Real Beauty Editor
American Girl
8400 Fairway Place
Middleton, WI 53562